Guess What

Published in the United States of America by
Cherry Lake Publishing
Ann Arbor, Michigan
www.cherrylakepublishing.com

Content Adviser: Susan Heinrichs Gray
Reading Adviser: Marla Conn, ReadAbility, Inc.
Book Design: Felicia Macheske

Photo Credits: © Michiel de Wit/Shutterstock.com, cover, 3, 21; © Roger de Montfort/Shutterstock.com, 1, 4;
© LorraineHudgins/Shutterstock.com, 7; tiverylucky/Shutterstock.com, 7; Bruce MacQueen/Shutterstock.com, 8;
© manfredxy/Shutterstock.com, 11; © Brandon Alms/Shutterstock.com, 12; © Gerald A. DeBoer/Shutterstock.com, 15;
© Chesapeake Images/Shutterstock.com, 17; © Jason Patrick Ross/Shutterstock.com, 18; © Eric Isselée/Shutterstock.com,
back cover; © Andrey_Kuzmin/Shutterstock.com, back cover

Library of Congress Cataloging-in-Publication Data

Calhoun, Kelly, author.
 Spotted singers / Kelly Calhoun.
 pages cm. — (Guess what)
 Summary: "Young children are natural problem solvers and always looking for answers, especially when it involves animals.
Guess What: Spotted Singers: Leopard Frog provides young curious readers with striking visual clues and simply written hints.
Using the photos and text, readers rely on visual literacy skills, reading, and reasoning as they solve the animal mystery. Clearly
written facts give readers a deeper understanding of how the animal lives. Additional text features, including a glossary and
an index, help students locate information and learn new words."— Provided by publisher.
 Audience: Ages 5-8.
 Audience: K to grade 3.
 ISBN 978-1-63362-630-0 (hardcover) — ISBN 978-1-63362-720-8 (pbk.) — ISBN 978-1-63362-810-6 (pdf) —
ISBN 978-1-63362-900-4 (ebook)
 1. Leopard frogs—Juvenile literature. [1. Frogs.] I. Title.

QL668.E27C34 2016
597.8'92—dc23

2015003101

Cherry Lake Publishing would like to acknowledge the work of The Partnership for 21st Century Skills.
Please visit *www.p21.org* for more information.

Printed in the United States of America
Corporate Graphics Inc.

Table of Contents

I have

eyes

on top of

my head.

My ears are flat and round.

My body is covered with slimy skin.

I puff up my cheeks to sing.

Yum! Yum!

I like to eat insects and worms.

I have
a big, wide
mouth.

I have legs made to jump and swim.

17

I like to hide from you.

Do you know what I am?

I'm a Leopard Frog!

About Leopard Frogs

1. A frog has smooth skin, which may feel slippery or slimy.

2. Frogs eat insects, worms, ants, flies, beetles, smaller frogs and even small birds.

3. Frogs have **webbed** feet to help them swim.

4. Baby frogs are called tadpoles.

5. A group of frogs is called an army.

Glossary

cheeks (cheeks) both sides of the face, below the eyes

insects (IN-sektz) a small animal with six legs and three main body parts

puff (puhf) to swell

slimy (SLIME-ee) wet, sticky and slippery

webbed (webd) having an area of skin between the fingers or toes

Index